Team Stats—Basketball Edition

MIAMI HEAT

Nicki Clausen-Grace
and Jeff Grace

BLACK RABBIT BOOKS

Bolt is published by Black Rabbit Books
P.O. Box 3263, Mankato, Minnesota, 56002.
www.blackrabbitbooks.com

Jennifer Besel, editor; Michael Sellner, designer;
Omay Ayres, photo researcher

Library of Congress Cataloging-in-Publication Data
Names: Clausen-Grace, Nicki, author. | Grace, Jeff, 1967- author.
Title: Miami Heat / Nicki Clausen-Grace and Jeff Grace.
Description: Mankato : Black Rabbit Books, 2021. |
Series: Bolt. Team stats, basketball edition | Includes bibliographical references and index. |
Audience: Ages 8-12 | Audience: Grades 4-6 |
Summary: "Discover the Miami Heat's powerhouse players and biggest moments through exciting text and dynamic infographics"— Provided by publisher.
Identifiers: LCCN 2019051126 (print) | LCCN 2019051127 (ebook) |
ISBN 9781623102937 (hardcover) | ISBN 9781644663899 (paperback) |
ISBN 9781623103873 (ebook)
Subjects: LCSH: Miami Heat (Basketball team)—History—Juvenile literature.
Classification: LCC GV885.52.M53 C53 2021 (print) | LCC GV885.52.M53 (ebook) | DDC 796.323/6409759381—dc23
LC record available at https://lccn.loc.gov/2019051126
LC ebook record available at https://lccn.loc.gov/2019051127

Printed in the United States. 2/20

All facts and statistics are current as of the 2018–2019 season.

Image Credits

Alamy: Roberto La Rosa, 3; Tribune Content Agency LLC, 14–15; UPI, 21; ZUMA, 22–23; AP Images: DUANE BURLESON, 10–11; Lynne Sladky, Cover, 4–5; Tim Johnson, 7; Tom DiPace, 24; TONY DEJAK, 26; Wilfredo Lee, 15; bleacherreport.com: Bleacher Report, 4–5; commons.wikimedia.org: BASS Tickets, 7; ebay.com: christinconagh0, 28–29; Getty: Gustavo Caballero, 16–17; Miami Herald, 13, 18–19; Newscom: JASON ARNOLD/KRT, 24–25; SB NATION: Steve von Horn, 8; Shutterstock: Duda Vasilii, 28–29; EFKS, Cover, 1; GOLFX, 31; IfH, Cover; vasosh, 6, 10–11, 19, 28–29, 32

CONTENTS

HEAT
6

On the COURT

It was Game 7 of the 2013 NBA Finals. The Miami Heat led the San Antonio Spurs by two points. With 27 seconds left, Heat player LeBron James sank a long jump shot. Those points **secured** the win. The team won its third NBA title.

History of the HEAT

The Miami Heat has been burning up courts since 1988. It won three championships in 25 years. Compare that to the New York Knicks. That team has two titles. And it's been around since 1946.

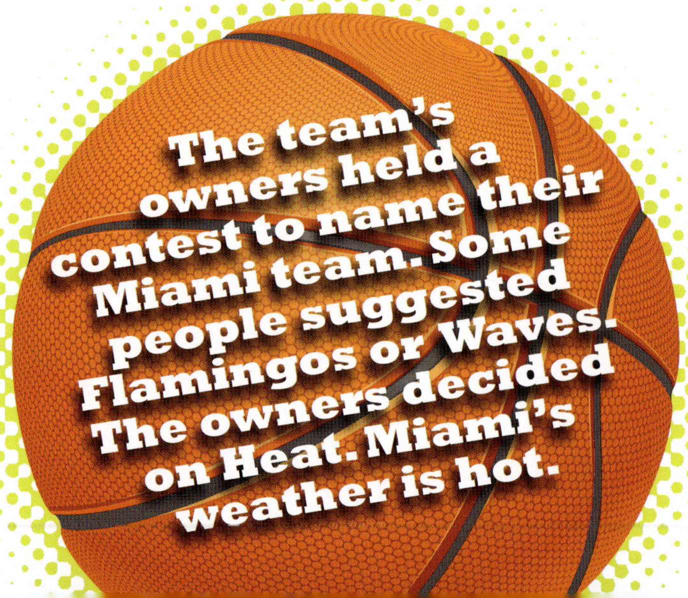

1988 team

CHAMPIONS
20 13
20 13

Making Money

Owners paid about $33 million in 1988 to start the team. In 2018, the team was worth $1.7 billion. This was the 10th highest in the NBA. Teams make money through ticket sales. They also sell items with the team **logo** on them. TV deals bring in the dollars too.

TEAMS WORTH THE MOST MONEY

NBA teams are worth a lot of money. A team's net worth is the money it would have after selling everything and paying all its bills.

$2.8 billion
$2.3 billion
$2.2 billion
$2.15 billion
$1.9 billion
$1.7 billion
Boston Celtics
Brooklyn Nets
Houston Rockets
Los Angeles Clippers
Dallas Mavericks
Miami Heat

CHAPTER 3

Greatest MOMENTS

The Heat has had some great moments. In the 2012 NBA Finals, it played the Oklahoma City Thunder. The Heat lost the first game. Then it caught fire. The Heat led Game 2 98–96. It had 7.1 seconds left. LeBron James grabbed the ball and then was **fouled**. James made both free throws. The Heat got the win. It went on to win the next three games and an NBA title.

OKC

HEAT

Setting Records

The best teammates play well under pressure. LeBron James showed he could do that. On March 3, 2014, James had a broken nose. He had to wear a mask to protect it. But he played through the pain and set records. He scored 61 points. It was his highest-scoring game. And it was the most points any Heat player had scored in a game.

The team mascot is Burnie. It is a fireball.

Chris Bosh

Good Picks

When teams **draft** good players, it's exciting. In 2003, the Heat drafted Dwyane Wade. Then in 2010, the team signed LeBron James and Chris Bosh. They teamed up with Wade. Together, they were called the "Big 3." They took the team to four NBA finals in four years. They won two NBA titles.

Big 3

Heat Team Records

By the Numbers

66
most **wins** in a season

126–83
score of biggest **win**

80–148
score of biggest **loss**

149 most points scored in a game

15 fewest wins in a season

54 fewest points scored in a game

CHAPTER 4

HEAT Superstars

Teams need people with **strategy** and skill. The Heat has had many great players and coaches.

Dwyane Wade played 15 seasons and 948 games with the team. He played in 13 NBA All-Star games. His talent helped the Heat win three championships.

MIAMI
3

Comparing Some Heat Players' Scoring Averages

LeBron James
26.9

LeBron James

Many people say LeBron James is one of the NBA's greatest players. He joined the Heat in 2010. With the team, he won two NBA titles. He is fourth in NBA history in points scored.

Dwyane Wade
22.7

Shaquille O'Neal
19.6

Chris Bosh
18.0

Shaquille O'Neal

Shaquille O'Neal is a big man. He is 7 feet, 1 inch (2.2 meters) tall. And he weighed 325 pounds (147 kilograms). O'Neal was hard to guard. Dwyane Wade loved to pass to him for slam dunks.

O'Neal wore a size 22 shoe.

Most NBA Career Coaching Wins

*still coaching

Pat Riley

Coach Pat Riley didn't start with the Heat. He coached the Los Angeles Lakers and New York Knicks first. He joined the Heat in 1995. Players **respected** him. He had helped the Lakers win four titles. He coached the Heat to its first NBA championship.

With great players and coaches, the Heat keeps games hot. Fans can't wait to see what it does next.

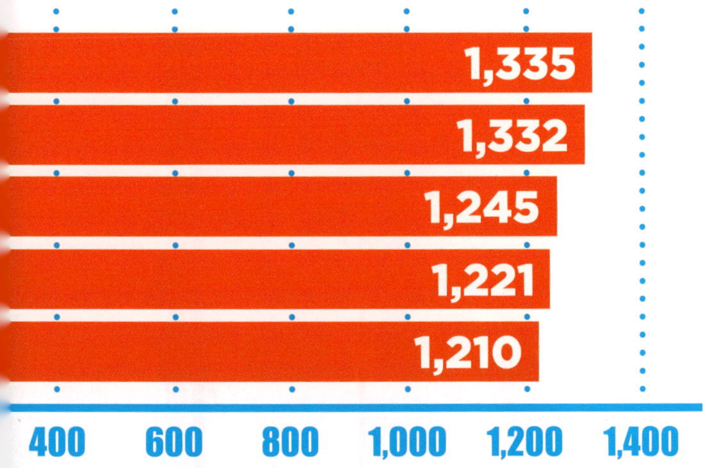

HEAT TIMELINE

1988

The team forms.

2003

The Heat drafts Wade.

2006 The team wins first NBA championship.

2012 The Big 3 lead the team to a second championship.

2013 Team wins third NBA championship.

2014 James scores 61 points in a game.

GLOSSARY

career (kuh-REER)—a period of time spent in a job

draft (DRAFT)—to pick a player for a professional team through a specialized system

foul (FAWL)—to do an action that is against the rules

logo (LO-go)—a symbol used to identify a company

mascot (MAH-scaht)—a person, animal, or object adopted by a group as a symbolic figure especially to bring them good luck

respect (REE-spekt)—to consider worthy of high regard

secure (suh-KEYR)—to make free from risk of loss

strategy (STRAH-tuh-jee)—a careful plan or method

BOOKS

Anderson, Josh, and Heather Kissock. *Miami Heat.* Inside the NBA. New York: AV2 by Weigl, 2016.

Gigliotti, Jim. *Miami Heat.* Insider's Guide to Pro Basketball. Mankato, MN: Child's World, 2019.

Whiting, Jim. *Miami Heat.* The NBA: A History of Hoops. Mankato, MN: Creative Education, 2018.

WEBSITES

Dwyane Wade—Biography
www.biography.com/athlete/dwyane-wade

Miami Heat
www.britannica.com/topic/Miami-Heat

Miami Heat
www.nba.com/heat/

INDEX